CARRIER WAVE

CARRIER WAVE

by JASWINDER BOLINA

Center
for
Literary
Publishing
Fort Collins

Printed in the United States of America.

Library of Congress Cataloging-in-Publication Data

Bolina, Jaswinder, 1978–
    Carrier wave / by Jaswinder Bolina.
        p. cm. -- (The Colorado prize for poetry)
    Includes bibliographical references and index.
    ISBN-13: 978-1-885635-09-9 (pbk. : alk. paper)
    ISBN-10: 1-885635-09-5 (pbk. : alk. paper)
    I. Title. II. Series.

    PS3602.O6538C37 2006
    811'.6--dc22

    2006020919

The paper used in this book meets the minimum
requirements of the American National Standard
for Information Sciences-Permanence of Paper
for Printed Library Materials, ANSI Z39.48-1984.

1 2 3 4 5   10 09 08 07 06

for my parents

After a while I understood that,
talking this way, everything dissolves: *justice,*
pine, hair, woman, you and *I.*

—Robert Hass, "Meditation at Lagunitas"

CONTENTS

((TWO

(((**THREE**

((((*

CARRIER WAVE

TRANSMISSION FROM HQ

Code 1: I kissed the elephant in the alley
behind my apartment. Code 2: My elephant Wanda.
                      Code 3: A malignancy has consumed
my elephant's recollection.
Code 4: My elephant cannot recall my name.

                      Code 5: Heisenberg, heisenberg,
visibility-in-principle. Code 6: In Knoxville they can't distinguish
the sulfur cloud from the fog. Code 7: I can't distinguish the road
from the sulfur cloud.
                      Code 8: I'm a traveling circus.

Code 9: Might I unload my habiliments in your tool shed?
Beside the defense mechanism? Code 10: Inside
your decoder ring? Code 11: Under your Rosetta stone.

Figure-me-loosely.

Code 12: Sometimes the stream circumvents the river
and engages the ocean directly.

Code 13: Many people will ask you how you're feeling.

But that's Knoxville for you. Have you ever been?
There's a diner there called Lorlene's.

When you arrive, Lorlene will ask: *How're you feeling?*

                  You'll respond: *Leaky Robot*
Toilet Training Nebulous Tree Wanda Why'd you leave

me at the bus stop your eyes resolute signposts?

You will hand Lorlene your briefcase and walk calmly
out the door. You will ignore what pursues you.

And if what pursues you does not wish to be ignored,
you will name it Ernie: It's easier to deal with what pursues you
if what pursues you is Ernie.   Rheostat. Bongo. Blip.   Blip.   Blip.

(ONE

POEM 70

(hello matchstick with your little hairdo
of flame)
             (hello red buds blooming)

The bones of the archaeologist were discovered today
by other, younger archaeologists (who'd been
looking for grander artifacts).

I drove the car past the dog beneath the catalpa tree, (voices in the head
of the car broadcast remotely, but)
        the dog didn't hear any voices
except maybe his own (which might've been calling out
his seven sisters lost
        among the little brats in want
of puppies of the world).

I scoured the oak molding (I stained the balustrade).

There's a lesson in the architecture
        but none of us who live here can quite get at it
                            ('it'

because) I'm thinking the unattainable might be
a nettle between the fingers (or a pyretic transistor,
        might be) a tactile
thing to be held and pored over.

The year is twenty-o-six. The time is eight-o-six.
O what light the mirror is wearing.

ONE OR TWO RUNS OF THE MILL BEFORE STUMBLING HAPLESSLY INTO THE FREAK SHOW

Before the initial conditions arrive at their interim conclusions
and begin to pupate,
it's all umbrellas, no corrosive rain.
All cocoon, no slithery beast emerging.
But eventually the happenings haywire. Moths
twitter after the light, the gooey light
squinting through the gravity lenses.
You put your ear to a window.
You hear its liquid coursing. Put your hand in a jar
and palpate its airy viscera.
You've forgotten to eat.
You need to catch a plane out of the city
except all the planes are headed to cities
forming a snarl of goings-on no one can conclusively untangle.
The skycap can tell you're pretty upset,
so he says for five bucks
he'll show you his bearded lady,
his riding mower with a two-bushel catch.
Inside your chest, a couple of wolves.
Inside this body, another body twitching.
A spider with its legs
wrapped around
the head of a dragonfly.

EMPLOYING MY SCYTHE

I'm standing in field 17 of the long series, employing my scythe.
Sometimes a conceptual dog bounds
past me, though it's never my conceptual dog.
Occasionally future laureates gather for colloquium,
though they're rarely my future
laureates. Thus, evening proceeds precisely
the way the handbook describes it:
as a proceeding: a runnel: shallow and babbling.

Into it a stranger appears. He looks like my friend.
I ask him, Are you my friend? Gravity telegraphs
its heavy message through the lolling
vines. The stranger says, I've sold all my clothes
and am considering, for a career, perpetual suffering.
The sun slides a tongue down the nape of the grain elevator.
Lowing cattle. It's the fourth of July. In Spain.
I say, You are most vague and mysterious, friend.
The dog paces. I set my scythe aside and tell him,
I have employed this scythe mercilessly all my life and still
everywhere these stalks extend. He says,
Someone is always worse off than us
even at our most pitiable. Yes, I say. I read it once
in a magazine. And we laugh, let our enormous bellies jangle.
It is good to laugh with my friend and let the scythe cool, I say.
Yes, he says. Good.

ALL THE HEXAGONAL FACES LILTING FROM THE CROWD

I've taken awhile to reply   to your telegram
of a fortnight ago.   Weeks pass as if they're
riding on trains.   The air softens.   Karen Siegel
walks into the lounge.   Speaking to her, I'm
ravished by my voice.   Does this ever happen
to you?   Echoes, a coffee can,   a string.
This probably never happens to you.   I hadn't
written,   though   I should've written.
How is life?   I prefer to not watch the doorway.
Certainly the weather.   I've forgotten to spell.
I'm out late drinking lime rickeys.   Often,
I repeat myself.   The air softens for this
I apologize.   I have been stolid,   un-running.
Saying hello,   to me,   sounds awful. I don't
believe in hell.   How's your grandmother?
Where are you now?   Karen says hello.
You   should   not   believe   her.

MIDDLE-AGED WOMEN DANCING TO COUNTRY MUSIC WITH NO SHOES ON

If you believe in consciousness
as emergent phenomenon,
it won't surprise you

fractals can reproduce a nimbus
resembling three bulbous horses
beaming in the slow wind.

If you don't believe in
consciousness as emergent
phenomenon, there's something
wrong with you.

Tonight, nothing but twang.

The bouncer not checking I.D.
at the barroom door, but don't
mistake this as an open invitation.

Take this as a muted understanding

as when an eyebrow's raised
or the long finger's pointed upward
in heavy traffic.

Your odometer still requires adequate mileage.
If you haven't been to Chattanooga, don't bother.

I spent late afternoon on the couch
in pajamas reciting. It was a slow day,

the splotchy undercarriage
of the eyelids taking on successive
shapes of a long-sunk goldfish,
the Zoo Lights of Lincoln Park,
and the numinous manhole geysers
of a wintered city.

A face appeared of the temporary

woman I hardly cared for except
in her rapid, predawn departures
when the outward force
of the suddenly spacious bed
vied with the density
of her absence, and the room
fell into silent equilibrium.

There's all what I can tell you.

All this venturing, and in speaking
it to you, the lion's dead
in my mouth when I'm saying *lion*.

In punting it aloft, the symbolic
lands short of its goalposts,

the signpost only understood
if it's visible through more than fog.

Still, the bunions of these women
percuss their telegrams
on a floor of warped wood

amid a recurring swoosh of dress hems
that are nothing like the tidal turns of the sea.

INTERRUPTED CONVERSATION PART 2

I'm among those oft cited tribes who believe photographs are purloiners of the soul.

In that case, I'd advise a lemon peel in carbonated water, Anichini advises. Is there anything that can't be cured with a lemon peel? asks Lynn. Rickets, Jorge replies.

Back then none of us is conceptual. Reduced by the verbiage or any kind of resonance imaging. Back then, it's all very real like a hangover or descent from a moment of unbearable clarity.

Paul states, There's no metaphysical necessity for a tea infuser. Michael adds resolutely, In experience, there is no resolution. Jeff mumbles, My mouth's a ball of twine. Tom says, The dead haven't changed their minds. But we're cautiously optimistic, offers Noah.

There's a bleating transistor in your chest. The sparrow doesn't see the window. Like electrons in close quarters, there's the inevitable colliding.

Anne asserts, You will end strangely. Not unlike a daring screen-adaptation of a lesser-known novel, chuckles Hoks. Antoinette concedes, You'll never find love that's both pure and deep, because anything that deep usually gets pretty murky.

You will not be alone, says father. But no one will really know you, adds uncle.

Then,   after years of wobbling,   the sun begins to wield us as symbolic imagery   which makes us   feel quite hollow and all beside ourselves.

FROM *THE TRACTATUS LOGICO-PHILOSOPHICUS,* UNABRIDGED

6.43   *If good or bad willing changes the world, it can only change the limits of the world, not the facts; not the things that can be expressed in language.*

6.4301   Some will suggest you shouldn't look out the window, witness the dissonance, and if you should look out the window, you can't convey what you find there.

6.41   *The sense of the world must lie outside the world. In the world everything is as it is and happens as it does happen. In it there is no value—and if there were, it would be of no value.*

If there is a value which is of value, it must lie outside all happening and being-so. For all happening and being-so is accidental.

6.411   Wrought iron and an awning, eucalyptus and the people beneath the awning who become paratroopers in any dream of paratrooping; filled with rocks imitating stones and stone-faced trees and tree-shaped bodies, every item is separate but included: the minerals, the ores, the ghastly carbons, one version of the Apocalypse in which the Chosen cross a bridge the width of a hair as the rest of us fall into the valley, one version of the valley in which all our hung days are fleshy and warm, and suffering's ironically clever. In one version of suffering, nothing is given or taken away.

5.1362   *The freedom of the will consists in the fact that future actions cannot be known now. We could only know them if causality were an inner necessity, like that of logical deduction.—The connexion of knowledge and what is known is that of logical necessity.*

5.13621   Possibility is retribution for freedom of the will. It's such a wide open pasture and the carnivorous beasts disjunctively lurching. Standing in a pasture, you find yourself ogled by eyes. The atmosphere a warped Plexiglas. Freedom of the will is the possibility of.

A man in the pasture. A shack, a path of white gravel, the palled horizon. The world decided as wax when wax is cool and hard. You offer the man a bowl. The bowl is filled with ice. He gives you a flower. You're standing in a pasture you assume resembles death in the sense of death as a pasture. Perspective is the conciliatory offering of the light. You're so rarely in a pasture.

6.431   *As in death, too, the world does not change, but ceases.*

6.4311   *Death is not an event of life. Death is not lived through.*

6.4321   Deadly nightshade, belladonna, bittersweet: a progression, though they all mean *solanum dulcamara,* which means if you ate the solitary, nodding, purplish-brown, bell-shaped petals or glossy black berries, it'd kill you. And without you, nothing much would happen.

FAST ACCESS

The fly is called Rhombus when the conditions are such that
                                        all flies are rhombi, but not all rhombi are flies.

                                The moment is only momentarily the red eye of the bull.
        Then, it gets stuck in the ointment.

        The composition of fog is a few milliliters
                                Hey, where'd you come from? and a couple centiliters
                Hey, where'd you go to?

            Here's a peanut.
The peanut resembles a mitochondria in shape, but it's not mitochondrial.

                                                Here's your cellular phone number
        with all its mitochondria intact but no peanuts.

        Once, I owned a bulldog. You owned a red Peugeot.

                                                Here's the fog.

            The mind is hinges entirely.

Well, hinges and knobs.   Behind this door is another,
                more rhomboidal door. *Come on in.*

You enter the house. You depart the house.
Hey, you left your finger in here.

Here's the fog that's nearly hollow.

Try lifting it over your head.

PROFANE PORTRAITURE

Sunday morning,

some of us entirely   transistor,   some of us the circuit breaker breaking.

Her hair is   a-brown-paint-been-poured-on-her   amidst the junk of the carport,

her button-down shirt,

an illegible latticework of surfaces

—if the painting is done by numbers,   the baubles will be arranged

in increasing orders   of magnitude.   Sprockets of a cat

perched among thrushes,   a tarp of heat,   the many points

of vanishing,   the woman clothed   and descending

the nude staircase,   each of her 18 heads   the color of differing

carbonic polymers.   She's my wife.

Isn't she lovely?

MEMO TO LONG LOST LOVE—WITH ROBOT

Have you read the Employee Handbook?
Certainly—and the sequel also—

I've spent many Months—in this Factory
operating—the Conundrum—
Though little—of my Work has been offered—
Publication in the significant—trade Journals of the Age—

Among the grander Schemata—
I must confess—my Sympathies lie
with the Antibiotic Movement—
Salt corrodes my Robot's tin Skin—

He's a good robot—stout and efficient—

My pocket Watch—is lost like a Tooth—
My Evening—a greased Carousel—

When my robot is upset he tells Me—
You hurt my Feeling—my heart is a Pump—

PRUNING THE DEAD TREE

For breakfast we eat English breakfast beans. She assures me,
If on this morning you've awoken with a dagger beneath your pillow,
it doesn't mean that you're unspeakably, undeniably, indefensibly guilty.

But the canary is missing.

And so the day begins in its bonnet of fog.
And so I suggest ignoring any larger conclusions until the smaller ones have strolled
the neural catwalks freely.

And if what you're looking for is distinct subject matter and a clear sense
of urgency,

I hope you won't mind me saying you're in the wrong aisle
and pretty much a goner.

At this late date, the eyewitness testimony clutters, advances from the left,
delivers with the right.

If a narrative appears, it's only the brief hump of some loch ness monster,
figment of a fig tree.

It's entirely possible
the canary's protons simply, clearly and urgently ruptured.

There's a reversal of shadows in afternoon. The glut of air traffic.
Revving machinery courses through the neighborhood.

I wear my old blue jeans, the ones you so admire
with their craters

and indefatigable creases which make me think of death
    which makes me think of an orgasm which makes me wonder which lasts longer.

I suggest you have to approach the ideas rapidly

                                        so as not to get tangled in their contrails.

                        You have to walk down the alleyway with a certain regard
for the junk heaped in dumpsters.

            You should understand that if you've looked through one window,
you've looked through the general idea of a window,
        although this claim is entirely conditional and doesn't apply to stained glass or lancets,

            so you have to repeat the procedure repeatedly.

        Today's tree, like yesterday's tree, is all angles and pears.

                            As always the door is the fat prong of entry,
but also the subtext of departure.

The lilacs, ravaged by an ice storm in early March, have blocked the passageway between
        houses, ours and the neighbor's,

and the list of chores includes "proceed with chainsaw."

It's over afternoon tea,
                    after the shadows have stood up and stretched their legs,
that she suggests, *If you're photonic, even mildly,*
                    you'll note that time progresses, but negligibly
        so that the canary goes missing,

                but missing like the pale branches of dogwood against
                            the usual pallor of April sky.

It's just an issue of contrasting.

                    Even when you're orphaned, your fingernails lurch
undetectably forward.
                Even now, you near a preliminary destination.

The lilacs three weeks short of blooming.

                            Pollen stored in the furtive pockets of the garden.

        In evening when her neck stands up on its shoulders and speaks volumes
    it does so with urgent clarity,
                    but the conversation funnels around the status of the day

which as it turns out is the secretive flap of a cat's tongue.

Clearly not everything is resolved.

There's still the issue with the dagger, the case of the missing canary,
that mention of an orphan in the twenty-third stanza,

and the question of whether the reader is the object of the direct address
or if the address is to the ambiguous woman who keeps
reappearing.

But right now, I'd prefer to discuss with you
my firm conviction that when the devil finally appears in the events of a novel,
it's always a bit of a letdown.

I'd like to say, *Lynch pins burgeoning in the architecture,*

and admit to you I often misread causal and casual
as in "Dress causally" or "causal sex" or
"Your unified field theory is, at end, casually inconsistent."

I would rather tell you that one need not mention
the transient nature of mist as transience
is an inherent feature within the nature of mist

much like the stone is within the rock
and the death within the orgasm
and the detailed historical account of events preceding
within the redundant rings of the tree.

She is numinous old leaves. A letter arrives.   It sits on a table
unopened for weeks.

MOOD RING

Inside me lived a small donkey. I didn't
believe in magic, but the donkey
was a sucker for the stuff. Psychics,
illusionists, arthritics who'd predict
the rainfall. That was the year I had trouble
walking. I over-thought it and couldn't
get the rhythm right. The donkey re-taught me.
"This foot. Yes, then that one. And swing
your arms as if you're going to trial
to be exonerated of a crime
you've most definitely committed."
Next, trouble sleeping because
I'd need to crank the generator in my chest
so frequently. Seeing I was overworked,
the donkey finally hauled it out—
it looked shiny and new, a silver dollar—
and tossed it into a flock of birds
who had to fly a long way to find safety.
I knew then I was a large and dangerous man,
what with this donkey living inside me,
but felt futile. One day, during
a final lesson on breathing,
the donkey asked what kind of jeans
I was wearing. I said, "The somber ones."
"Poor kid." "So will you be staying on
for a third year, donkey?" "No. I think
I should be leaving soon. I think
I should go and await your arrival beside
the crumpled river." "Yes, I suppose
you have many important matters to attend to,
but maybe one day I will come and join you
for a drink or, perhaps, for a brief nap."

BLUE PRINT MOUNTAIN

No stalactite not threatening

the floor. No missals on

erosion. No, not much

confluence in the architecture.

Because the mountain is young

in mountain years

it thinks itself treacherous.

Its hand made

of a kind of nitrate

used primarily in Western cautery ritual

which makes it difficult walking

the mountain home.

Your mother is a plate, Mountain!

Rain perforates. Your faces

are shrink-wrapped by the cloud

shapes: air bag, parachute,

apologia. When I open you up,

one thing drooping,

one thing on a string.

24

AUTO IMMUNE

Had I the time or intelligence with which to ruminate upon the little pulsar of the soul—

had I but trussed the tin ceiling

most maladies can be prevented through careful diet and regular exercise

but to believe that

most of the time coyote could clear the canyon if only he didn't look down

but he does look down

which is why I love him still

his face composed of triangles

so large the mail slot of the eye

so small the parcels it receives

the particulate skin

so negligible so

you'd never notice

underneath nakedness are reciprocating cylinders

the pistons pushing air

the heart chuckles on

electrically regulated and alternating

between open and closed

for blood to flow to the deeper strata

and underneath the deeper strata there's a mechanical turtle
or footprints of the turtle

he's the little turtle of my soul

but also a dark meat
aperture

a tin shack collapsing

most of the iceberg is underwater

mostly, the engine runs on air

—I would tell you I believe in none of its radiant charm.

GAUCHE, I REPEATED

And this signaled turbulence, rough water, gauche. Gauche, it echoed
remote and undersea. I didn't struggle for meaning: din of a crowd
gathered, a leaf, a zephyr, many motors on an avenue. Gauche,
offered the faucet flushing, tin foil arcing the microwave, air
as it rushed out over a tongue recalling then releasing me.
My name mimicked crumpling aluminum. Gauche, I repeated
knowing this meant something other but felt like applause,
how a tire in rainwater makes applause. How after her strokes,
my grandmother's breathing sounded like a word foreign to her
that sounded like breathing. For a month I drank only water.
Sunk pennies in the well of the ear, canals in the soft cartilage.

BY THIS TIME CZECHOSLOVAKIA IS REUNITED AND CALIFORNIA HAS FALLEN INTO THE SEA

Sunny days are Wednesdays. We contend we're alone, but the flagpole knotted
to the sky. The spiral staircase is the DNA of the home. *Here's your jet pack,*
you say. *Time to take a ride.* My watch face turns its face to face me, and we're in all
agreement. Time for a ride. But I go nowhere, arranging instead for the post to bear
mutely the owed and offered. My hand clears the supper table of complications.
The house captures air and we fill the air with fragrances. Withering pines. Smell
of dried flowers. We weave carpet and tread there. Dread-locked as it is, it holds us,
our lumbering. Now the weather makes the news. Weather, welcome to the center
of our attention. I will share with you my patient's ills. I wear you to my wedding.
I'll wear you when my batteries fail, when my prostate swells and my children say,
We hate you who never cared for me. The rooster at sunup crows. I lunge at it
with a stone. The rooster flies into the sea. I won't wake up again. I won't wake
the children. The children, godless, vacant and godless. Look how I pollute them.
Fit them with magnets, they repel each other. At funeral, they stick their fingers in
their noses and sully their dresses in cemetery mud. Start off the new year with sex
in the old bed. Close one eye, silhouette the woods. I don't describe the divine
describes us. The children, pulling dandelions up by the throat and gifting them to me.

BROKEN RADIO BELTWAY, ABRIDGED

18 January 1929:
My dearest Lydia,
God has arrived.
I met him on the 5.15 train.

— John Maynard Keynes

22.

and there were so many hours between exit ramps
      I drove my rig best I could without sleeping
            and that burger I ate earlier certainly
isn't sitting right in my stomach
               though it seemed like a good idea at the time
And at the time I said I would take back my mistakes if that would make your evening

At the time I said many things
      only half of them were true

            but then I   un der st o

27.

          The voice of God saying
          I've been here for hours not getting bored
              not thinking about you
              or not saying it
          the hours chuggle along

          And for some of you
               morning arrives easy
              but for some of us
          morning is the blunt end

29.

What with all this road-going and static   on the CB
there's no one here to talk to   And inside me
                                  there's nothing
                                  but sizzle
                                  and

33.

        The voice of God saying
                    I wish I was a spaceman
but my peepers were shot early on
              so this odometer is an orchid
              this road a black magic

35.

                        marker with which the astronomer diagrams
                              the universe
                on the stretched surface of a balloon
                    and the voice of God says

you should inflate the balloon

                                by whispering into it

38.

      Because within the I-beams of this world there are
          the T-beams
          of another world
          emerging

41.

      You should not ululate   Though these days I've become a little hard of hearing
and I'm generally uneasy
                and it seems no one makes a sound
                    what with all this road-going
     and the voice of God saying

42.

              I'm afraid of monsters

              So I drove my rig the many hours between exit ramps
              best I could without sl e ep i

44.

And the voice of God saying this world must be full of rigs rumbling past so
     the next one will seem less treacherous in its construction

The voice of God says
I guess I should've made the better choices
cut out the filler

48.

But everything gets tangled in
    because even barreling down the beltway
is nothing less than

50.

                The voice of God saying I do not forgive me
                The voice of God saying I don't believe in

                This sunburn makes
                my left arm look positively
                radi o ac t iv

51.

Illuminated by the dash light   I'm looking back on my life
                        as the trailing bulk of large machinery

57.

Because this world is something less than exquisite

58.

And I can see right through you

59.

                And whatever I say

                       will come to pass

                every way of life ending every

TWO

REPLY TO HQ

these details from the broad panoply:

Chester's brother blinded by staring at fireflies en masse.
Evergreens beside the house reminding Rita of Rita's mother
but not in any metaphoric sense.
And Abigail once telling me her second husband
brushed his teeth before going to the dentist making their entire marriage seem redundant,
repeated, reiterated.

These people know things about each other you wouldn't want to know.
There's a tussle here you wouldn't desire to be a part of:

Rita running on screaming Rita's mother's dead.   Chester's brother in the sanitarium.

It was Chester's agoraphobia what sent him to the loony bin.

And Abigail often says every girl in this place is in love with me,
and her brief stint with the psychic hotline makes me wonder.

I'm opening a paint can with a flathead screwdriver. The paint can is the metaphoric sense
of the girl, etcetera. World, etcetera. Etcetera, etcetera

INSPIRED BY ACTUAL EVENTS

While walking through the Tulley Street Gardens, I encountered a woman wearing what looked like an evening gown but less condescendingly so. She said nothing then disappeared behind a shrub. *Oh,* I thought, only then having noticed the gorgeous shrubbery strewn about. Historically, this was during more of a transitory period. Between the War and the parade celebrating the War. A lot of us had been volunteering on the cellblocks. I was on D where most of the guys read Foucault. They seemed a pretty sardonic bunch. One of the girls from C-block said they'd built busts of the presidents out of toothpicks. At recess we'd toss around ideas on what to do if left as the last person on the planet. Donna said that'd never happen to her as she'd never been late to roll call and didn't intend to be anytime soon. The scenario seemed more plausible in my case as I was famously tardy. So I suggested I'd deface the paintings of Max Ernst. No one wants to see a painting by Max Ernst in perfect solitude. It'd remind you too much.

NOTES FROM THE OUTFIELD

I. We're bored, and there are too many gnats, distance deceptive

    A. as to a moon fattened on the horizon, a skull reflective

        1. I sort of knew him once, Horatio. But here we are far from home, our passports expired. Oh bother. Who needs a safari? The plumbed and seeded hours. The windmill manufactures no wind. The map factory unmoving, suborbital

            a. as a bolt, a screw, scrap the astronaut abandoned in transit, a claim

                i. Been here. Been here too many hours over this stuck turf.

NEIGHBORHOOD WATCH

What varieties of tea do you offer?
O, y'know.

Casper walks into the hut and is proffered:
Earl grey, chuckles, chamomile,
afternoon tea and biscuits.

Paul and Angela is not available.

Jonah's sister is a villain.
Jonah's brother is a donkey's drooping gait.

Do you know Genevieve?

I often lounge around
and listen to the crooning
of our life and times.

The compacted units.
The impenetrable whole.

We are beneath a balcony.
We're under a balcony.

We don't understand each other entirely.

But the feeling of the light is
like warm water running
delicately down
one's buttocks.

Then Ralph opens his mouth
and purple ribbons flail out.
We call him in,
call him chum.

There's bracken in the hall
alongside the slew.
Patty replies,
staring at her shoe,

This bone might be housing for a filament.
But you wouldn't be able to read by its dead light.

Casper meets a woman once.
She looks like an elderly Joan of Arc
or a young Genevieve.

He often says he's headed
to the Governor's mansion
but spends the afternoon instead
in Kirsten's boudoir.

Not the Kirsten you know.
A different one.

I. FAMOUS LAST LINES

… Run the bath, Babette. I am coming in
From out of the driving maelstrom

… And if nothing should change, at least this day
Hasn't ended in some slaughter

… Evening approached politely
In its tired old coat, insisting

… My most loyal and unwitting friend, you.
Your face grew an obscure face

… It seemed then that the world might conclude succinctly
We ran out to buy a wool hat

… Rodents began stampeding
Fat clouds dropped sinister knickknacks

… Alfred looked on with a sublime sense of grief
Which made him look like a frond

… Though not literally. This was during
The Year of Stop-and-Go Traffic

… You handed me an unfinished kumquat.
The roadway went numb

… It seemed then the world might end like a trail
Curled into itself like a spoon

Gentle but inexhaustible zephyr.

II. LINES FROM A POEM

In the Month of the Lackadaisical Jaguar

When the hunt falls victim to inclement weather

Alfred tracked the migratory path of a vesper sparrow

A grey cottage outside New Buffalo

The trail runneth into

A plate glass window

Where the bird falls to a patio

Ants devoured the placid body

In a festival he followed closely

A week in January

The bird disappears completely

Save the outline of bones

Only faintly recalls bones

The way the aroma of triple sec

Recall a dead uncle

The day drew long as the half-life of a radioactive isotope

Long as wind

Long as we get soused

The temporal disparities of the landscape will be resolved

Everything natural and serene

But serenity plagues him

He runs out with the platoon on furlough

Finds himself in a yonder

A strip joint in Budapest

Reviewing plans for a new radar evasive catapult

With a prostitute whose vulva certainly is

Swollen fruit of an ancient mango tree

And a bit of a flophouse

His uvula quivers frenetically

The spleen puts in late hours

Music fills the vast

By now

Babette is seated in a nook of the green restaurant

Delighted by the piquancy of the house jam

Alfred gnaws delicately

In the nothing that has happened in days

It seems literally

With some relief

At least no one hath been struck by a moving van in the late hour

Which sounded so lovely

I thought it was you, he says

And they lay intricate plans down

A tree loaded with newborn mangoes

His soused hair dangles with droplets over his face

If you have the chance, why don't you stop by

The War

We have drink specials

Running on ironic twists, says Babette

Seeing his manifold faces

Like reflections in old aluminum

The photomicrograph doth witness thy blunders

My oldest and dearest friend

You have your weaknesses

but these are not the worst of you she says

She says the truth is a blinding

And the cost of a working Theory of Everything

Spend your life led by a dog

May lead you to a mango tree

Though the dog doesn't know you

Your many inquiries

Nothing you can recall

Not at a moment's notice

III. OPENING GESTURES

What ornament of animal suffering inside the slick
hump of a bird? I completed lunch as though
it were an equation. . . With tremendous difficulty. . .
The platter loaded with hollow bones. . . My husks
scattered among the peanut dust of the world. . .

I kept wishing you'd appear suddenly out of the immense
empty spaces between highway exits. . . Like a predator
upon fallen hatchlings. . . Or grief. . . And when you did
not, I began telling a story. . . I began telling it slowly. . .
With the patience of air attempting some erosion. . .
It began with rasping footsteps on the worn floor
of the many cramped saloons. . . It began in a room
surrounded by doors. . . All the valuations of a room…

Babette laid her parka in a corner of the restaurant. . .
Alfred had a beer and walked out into the street. . .
Everything had the quality of being familiar. . .
Though these were not people I knew
or their friends. . . It was New Year's Eve. . .
The Festival of Recurrence. . . Some leaves fell. . .
She brandished a dagger. . .

AND I DISBELIEVING

The week the power outed,   I could make out bellyaching men   drunk at dusk on Listerine
grinning at their reflections   in windows of the closed taverns,   the devils I didn't believe in.
I could make out the composition   of a photograph irradiated   all day by sun
on the dashboard   and losing its composure.   Faces, my own and the people I knew,
I could not believe   appeared in the ragged surfaces of masonry,   and in the   broken
dark   above the fused city,   I could make out an aurora,
so by daybreak,
I began to demand so much more from the sky;

not the Rorschach clouds   or deaf thunder,   not the industrious rain.   I demanded
more than the ruddy hue like walls of a crematory,   *Means good sailing weather,*
Sara would say   though she'd never been sailing,   so I didn't believe
her face a still surface wanting more   than a disruptive hailstorm   of disbelief
or morning.   But by then, it was morning,   and I began my early work,
listing like a car   whose pilot at dawn has drifted   seamlessly into sleep dreaming
the steering wheel is the smooth rail of a clavicle,   the spectacular departure.

ETHIC, RANT ETHIC

I believe only strumpets know the fallibility of mistrust.
One night, one of the ones I knew up and drove her Passat
off of Craven Bridge. I missed her, but knew she'd return,
undamaged, unrecognizable save a dimple in her chin.

Alone now, the mattress feels lumpy like a stranger's
sleeping beneath the sheets beneath me. I love myself,
but not like a stranger could. Especially one who offers
glass beads and Milky Ways in the playground.

Do I know this isn't a simple kindness? Why do I suspect
the stranger's trench coat? After all, he sleeps beneath me
and doesn't stir.

In the city we live like this. Porch upon porch upon.
We despise each other evenly. Vigilant when the power fails,
we call to one another assuring none have abandoned
their posts, no one is lost and approaching.

IN THE FILM VERSION

Everybody injured is put on   the angry medicine,
the kind you'd only take if the army boys forced you.

For this reason   I feign no great injury,
though the injuries are severe,

the kind you'd call circus variety   if somebody asked you:
large and impressive   even to a kid at the circus.

I wear headphones everywhere   which makes the folks
passing seem somewhat   out-of-sync with each other.

The street is in b-minor,   small and meek:
a cat rubbing up against your leg,   that sound

your mother makes   when you're falling down the stairs.
It's all a bit unsettling,   as when someone uses the word *sanctity*

in broad daylight,   and my recurring dream lingers
on the end of the world.   I know it sounds grandiose,

but eventually that world ends and the dream stops returning.
Then, the dream is stepping into the bathroom

to shave my face,   to wash my hands and dry them.
A friend says   this should be reason enough to send me

howling to the nuthouse.   A friend insists one kind of cicada
is asleep in every tree.   A friend tells me one kind of fruit fly

makes tiny combat with every kind of spider.

And the clouds hold   resolutely still, but anyone
can see they're dying   to give something up.

WHAT AWAITS THE THUNDER

Is a decided stillness, a silence that could overwhelm the artillery,
though the war wears on unflinching. I turn to you and say,
It's so difficult to be in love in wartime. We view no photographs
of the dead, but bombers dive like whales in the sky. I pursue them,
their symbolic, their metonymic until you tell me, *Knock it off,*
until it becomes so difficult to behave myself. The telephone whimpers
in disconnecting. Our ears in silence hang like sails in no wind. I grow
blind in one eye, we sleep beneath a palmetto, our legs overlapping
in a too warm bed until you kick me. In morning, news
from the front dribbles thick milk into the dishes of satellites,
and we sip from these without any idea what the clamor is about.
We only want them to forgive us and send coffee beans.
This reminds you of a story in which the father says,
What happened before won't ever happen again,
and tearfully, the boy accepts this, because he desires so much
to accept and forgive and embrace his father again. By then,
he's a grown man and isn't ashamed of openly weeping.
I weep openly and sight returns to my bum eye. The garden grows
stereoscopic in the murky and shuddering light. A familiar
anxiety disperses, and a new anxiety resounds in its place.
I feel claustrophobic in the hailstorm. I grow murderous in the fog.
You say knock it off. I say it's so difficult to be in love.

THE SPY EXPERIENCES BLOODLUST

Low-lying stratus clouds skew
a view of the celestial.

The lake gurgles with fractions and erasing.

I haven't yet learned 'celestial'
in the local language;

it's a buzz-saw of a word.

Too early in the evening, I think
for the slaughter.

But tug up the windows and in rush the moths.

Settle down, boy, settle down,
insists the heather.

And wishing no harm upon anyone,
I make time for this and for that

until even these desert me.

ACCOUNT OF THE NOTHING REMARKABLE

We must've been in the pub seated or
on the couch discussing with leash and dog
going out for a walk, taking in the
cold front battling the warm front, occluded.

Little the news day had to offer us
those days when your hair was buzz-cut-prickly
and my purview mostly included
a view of the situated comedy

of working and living together in
a humorous way. Everyone welcomed
and threw trinkets at us. The ottoman,
stout and crouching, cradled your clodhoppers,

laced up my corset, held our heads when we
felt upended, though this rarely happened
to us, the critical gaskets,
us little ripples in the difficult

construction of water. I pertinent
and you pertinent, neither deluded
nor feeling not deluded,
but perhaps only a tad out of sorts.

The dog wasn't even a dog, but a
soldier of the cavalry on leave; I,
a television repairman; you, a
dust buster. And none of us with much to

do Sundays or Tuesdays, so in the pub
we would sit, slurping our B-52s,
examining the cancan dancers for
palm olives, dust mites, strategic

intelligence, proclaiming to ourselves:
At least we're not floating stupidly
on the surface of a pond! At least the
city's still standing. Yeah, and at last

the rolling pin of dusk will come flatten
the shadows along the long haul of the bulwarks.

WHAT BECAME OF AMERICA

Months later, we thought we saw her at the Rumpus Room or the Elbo Room or the Long Bar
dangling off a barstool with a chrome-haired Belgian in town on merger talks.

By the time we got a little closer they'd left, no doubt for the Red Line or the Green Mill
or the Rhythm Room.

Though most of us were sober and quite farsighted, I insisted this was not America.

I remembered the pale-years-ago light between storms in May when I'd lie with my hand on her
belly, soft, flat, dressed with silken hairs. She claimed she'd take a bullet for me.

Cellophane day, brambles under a steep light blooming, bouquets in the cemetery vivid
as lit kerosene, I fancied flowers freshly bursting from my chest. I imagined feeling
quite like myself again.

Hours later, I awoke to find she'd raided the fridge and pantry. She'd taken her lipstick and gone.
America at daybreak stepped out in an evening gown and hung a Ricky at the corner of Ashland
and Racsher, left us all wondering what became of America.

Lately, I wander down to the corner, sit on my rock, and puff a cigarillo. I listen hard
to the industrious sex of others roil down through the open windows. I daydream a novel,
my heroine with a toothache. I mistake the bodies passing for bodies familiar.

Once, I think I spot America smoking a roach in front of Andy's Gyros, but it's only
a neighborhood kid not speaking, not playing baseball.

EN ROUTE TO ASSASSINATING THE SECRETARY OF DEFENSE

I'd been absent too long to remember the harsh
sentence of arrival. I'd understood little but knew
to go home and pleasure my wife.

Her smile would break: a ribbon,
the ribbon strewn across a pile of tires,
the tires set on fire.

There are vapors in the city that will linger
for years. I inhaled their combustion
while departing. Returning now, they greet me.

I move on foot down avenues between
things and the names of things:
litter in its stance of collecting, lumber

for the kindling, a butcher's son,
his family gathered for the cortege
and preparing his body on a counter

in the deli. Posed with a flower, he looks dressed
for an interview. His soldiering days over,
his rations age and sour.

I'm desperate and untenable,
approaching, sanctioned and lethal,
on a glass elevator to the executive suite.

Illuminated by the fiber optic, approaching
on a glass elevator to the executive suite,
luminous and consumed.

THE SPIDERS THAT LIVE IN MY APARTMENT

I do battle with

    who build their huts

        and villages

    in corners

        along the ceiling

    Make no funny faces

        I approach

with shoe cocked

        or vacuum hose

    like walking through steam

walking with that much grace

Nightly, the Speakers speak softly

       beyond the last belt loop of the orange city.

        One asks, *Is the world a derangement*

001   010010100100   1010010100100101001

of Other? The other replies,

      Would you suggest it so? A third adds, *Harrumph.*

A sky is there, city an intrusion.

          00101001   10010010100101001

The Tanner stumbles into a carriage house.

     He's in pursuit of his chums who've enlisted

   and will be shipped out in the morning.

       He'll spend the War in quiet isolation,

0010100101001001010   0101001001010010   1001

strolling often past the bank building

    through the alternating light and lack of light.

00101001111001101010100101001001010   0101001   0010100
01011001100001001001010100101110010010010000010010010100100101110010010010010010011001000010010010010010011100100101001001001001011001000010
1001011100100101001010010010110011000010010010100100101110010010

59

I'm stranded in the trolley station.   I am stoned, fair weather,

on a pier beneath a blue shore light.

00101001010010010100101001

The sun is shrapnel launched at the opposing horizon.

The moon pummels the water to chalk.

0010100101001

I conquer my fear of heights standing on a mirror.

This is after the Great War is preempted

001010010100100101001011   001

by the Only So-so Ones.

Grass wavering in the panting field,

I'm deadened by the yearning an entire field is capable of,

and I feel compelled to say many things

but all at once like a turbine.

00101001111001101010100101001001010   0101001   0010100
0101100110000100100101001001011001001010010000010010101001001011100100101001010100100101100100001001001010010010111001001010010010010110011000010
1001011100100101001001001001011001100001001001010010010111001001 0

This is in ought-two among static transmissions.

In ought-two,

the Citizenry puts its boots on and goes parading.

00101001 10010   010100101001

I contend every catastrophe begins locally before debuting

in the larger theater,

0010100101001001   010100101   010100101   0100101001

and the locals are gathering their quivers and bows.

At the Front, one of the Tanner's chums is dismembered

during an extended cannonade.

001010010100

Her limp limb is hung from a bridge.

The Citizenry weeps because the Other is not an idea.

00101001111001101010100101001001010   0101001   0010100
0101100110000100100101001001011100100101001000010010010100100101110010010010010100100101100110000010
1001011100100101001001001001011001100001001001010010010111001001001010010010010110011000010
1001011100100101001001011001100001001001010010010111001001001010010010010111001001001010010010010111
001011100100101001010010010110011000010010010100100101011001100001001001010010010101110010010

When we're mug to mug, I wonder what you'd look like in theory.

0010100110100100111010010100100101001 0101001

In theory, weird Other, you'll be rewarded for your suffering

though not in a way I can conjure.

Your face in strings, the air is awful

0101001010010010100   101001

until I think of all the lovely folks

001010010100   1001   0100101001

willing to pull over to the curb for an ambulance

and feel exquisite.

00101001111001101010100101001001010   0101001   0010100
01011001100001001001010010010111001001010010000100101010010010111001001001001010010010110011000010010010010010010111001001010010100100101100110000 10
1001011100100101001010010010110011000010010010100100101110010010

The Tobacconist and Apothecary assemble their chessmen

between fractal patterns of disaster.

The Apothecary exposes his king's rook entirely.

0010100101001001   0100101001

62

A knight approaches in torqued advances.

This is the little metaphor for war,

is the idea of disputing factions

hurling consequences at each other.

But when all at last is lost,

00101111001010110100101011110010100101001001   0101

the Tobacconist buys the Apothecary his beer,

and the Biochemical Engineer embraces his lover,

and some weeks pass, and the Venture Capitalist

rents a party tent and throws a party.

00101001   0100   10010100101001

The Virgin carries Her Lame Husband in on her back.

The Dilettante arrives unmarried, but with all his limbs attached.

00101001010   01

A sky is there, is scenic overlook.

The Pardoner tells his tale to the Deputy Commissioner of Expired Motifs,

and the party's a riot, so they shatter some china.

Elsewhere, others are landing heavily in thatch.

0010100111100110101010010010010010   0101001   0010100
0101100110000100100101001001011100100101001000010010010100100101110010010100101001001001011100100101001010010010110011000010
1001011100100101001010010010110011000010010010101001001011100010010

In the late aboveground, the sky is an orange coat nightly.

There's static on the radio

0010100101001001010   0101001001010010   1001

and successive trains rattling.

The Standard Federal Bank building smites the ground it stands on

but for a period of decades,

0010100   101001

so the ground grows quite accustomed,

so the Butcher about his daily butchery hasn't noticed any affliction.

So and so and so on,

I propose the world is consecutive thump.

001010010100   1001   01001   01001

There's the bristling chill, bristling pines, bristling notion anything can be compacted, lit, and launched at a wall.

I propose I am pure concoction.

When the air raid sirens suggest it's time we had an air raid,

0010100101001

the city through the night scope emerges in an emerald haze,

emerges as a vision of the green night of the Other.

And, I don't believe in the War,

but when you don't believe in the War,

00111110100101001

you go on buying lunch meat.

You go on believing vinyl siding will protect the hut in severe weather.

You hope the ambulance will be your good horse

in cases of emergency.

00101001111010010011110100101001

I spend six hours in the refinery and don't find a hint of refinement.

I saunter down the pier and find the city digging its toes in.

The view from the scenic overlook is entirely overlook.

To the wrecking ball, it's all job opportunity.

0010100111100110101010010100100111001010   0101001   0010100
010110011000010010010100100101110010010100100001001001010010010101110010010010010010010100100101110010010010010010011001000010
1001011100100101001010010010011001100001001001010010010101110010010

The Mayor's Second Wife knits cozies for the ammunition depot.

The Radiologist sleeps, the Sergeants at Arms get soused,

0010 100101001   0010100101001
awnings yawning.

The Organ Pipe Repairman repairs the Beekeeper's organs

while the Lovers are lovingly shrugging.

I stumble down a fractal edge of the city.

0010100111100110101010010100100111001010   0101001   0010100

Palmettos prepare to break open and spill their internal contraptions,

parachutes unfurling into the countless mouths of the sky.

There's the not-quite-liquid of some you.

0010100101001

There's the slow grinding end of a world.

The War consumes the town and by the time the ref calls it,

there are only the two of us left standing,

00101001   0100

though we don't resemble each other.

Dearest Other, I'm beside myself when I'm beside you.

Deliberate Other, I've taken so much from you,
I'm unable to forgive your intrusion.

Delicate Other,
If you've ever thought of yourself in terms of *Self-portrait in Robe*

with Axe
or imagined the perfect method for the disposal of a body,

0010100   1010011001100110011001100110100110011

you may know a little of what I mean0010100

001010010100
    001010010100
001010010100
    001010010100
001010010100

00101001

THREE

OPERATING DICTATES FOR A PARTICLE ACCELERATOR

i.   pulse light

starts there starts   getting smaller   All that you can't remember,
Claire says. , With two glass eyes   I'm wobbling down
   a walkway   inflecting aloha   no thumbtacks,
        attached   no pins,   To feel.   Good by.
among crimson and silver turnstiles,   all the folks   In orange,
        Silvery hats and thermal   The madmen mad getting
madder   daisies all done   Again   me strolling, me fuming,
slipping, the stream frozen. the matter of fact. The quasars

   huffing on.   In December   no summery mask,   No, just
the shimmering scene, the firmament.   a blackbird indicating, nods
        Maybe a change   dust of a brick maybe
I remember,   I recall.   a cyclotron.   An ingenuous ramrod
    The flay of her hair   fall sinking   Rowboat
turning to winter,   rowboat, rowboat   Chatter of the breakage

iii.   verb forms of a neutron bomb

     starts sloe gin   over time   Fermenting in the firmament
       red shifting with Claire   waking with Claire, betweening
and vaguing Claire   the embassies exchanging airs.   lily white,
    glittery photons   , spark   at the bottom working
iamb   iamb iamb   iamb   iamb
Claire   don't care   reminiscing   Tuscaloosa
in.   A corner of the soiree.   , standing so bluntly
    you resemble no one,   Precisely. as if receding   over a hill,

you resembles everyone. corralling   , the bulky idea of the hill into.
     an encampment,   a tiny cranium.
  And it's   as if,   Spying you   through
    a whiskey on rocks.   a mass hysteria
I struttle along,   Making   commonplace.   Ubnutterances,
    and guts   your house is blue with two glass eyes

iii.   quantum entanglement

starts with a single shot.   fired   not the year of my   fathers.
    slow, death starts.   year my mother goes   terminal,
The vacuous scene   chattering,   Like an elephant
   collapsing   the animals fuming,   weird winged bugs
    The serious business of.   squishing them, they simply regroup.
And reappear. , Claire.   I'm stumbling down the thoroughfare.
in a dark, Pinching what few glittering photons,   I'm trolling.
murky and building up.   start at the bottom,   working a way

Upwards   Evening,   like a tumbler.   folding. itself over
       Feeling contented all around. squinting,   started clawing
with two glass eyes   feeling for thumbtacks.   Among
the broad vagaries.   among the wild visions,   Claire.
. I say I know you better,   , than. You could imagine,
      or some other,   but you sock me.   Hard. In the gut instead.

i.   aimed by magnets

            starts redundant   Futile with a screwdriver, among the wrecks.
   , I am having a ball comma   Describe the house   comma paint
   the doorjamb end-stop   these months   spent   a-chatter.
            the sidewalk spinal column   of a mule that carries me.
   Through the broad making-world.   one universe over,   ,
   We are inseparable.   And own many cats   the city.   Large.
     like viewing an egg,   From the egg's interior.
   I go about the serious business   strolling,   The firmament

   Claire. your pocket watch,   A frayed yellow.   T-shirt.
   on the narrative fringe. of the narrative,   the weightless photons
   say   Holding hands   One universe over. You do not forgive
     me.   , all that I can't   but Maybe a small change
   maybe something less   than the sky,
        maybe something.   More than the sky could conjure.

ii.   if this were a sonnet, I

                start with all that you can't remember.   The gutters
Overloaded.   the funky trinkets,   Weird winged bugs
 on the sill.   In the air,   When I go about the   business
, strolling home Claire.   riding the slipstream
sloe gin.   All drink and whiskey.   the old ferry, a rowboat
,   in my gut.   smooth as a mirror   Every mad
Artifact   everyone I've ever met,   resembling
Claire dissembling   My wintered axe.   start at the bottom

Work your way upwards.   like a signature saying I've been here,
  strolling past,   these fumes,   on the air
smell like a letter.   All thermal   , all watery Quasars
  bleating,   blackbird saying, The search light pauses   Pluck
The wings out one at a time.   Chicago and   blackbird, blackbird,
I unaware.   of ours, the   recombinant bodies of the gods.

i.   focused by a lens

starts with the scene   starts.   December,   Smooth
as a mirror   Hard in the gut   ,   feels like a tumbler.
        Claire, inflecting   good, by.   walking.
Claire.   the scene of sparks.   among the while, the fission
   The house is blue.   with two glass eyes   among the firmament

no pins to pin you No, thumbtacks to hold you   But photons and
     all the things that you can't   .   Among the sloe gin,
your frayed yellow T-shirt. I returned   to you, but you wanting

In a corner of the soiree. a corner of the prairie,   more than the sky
  This is where the elephant toppled.   when what you remember is
Collided, with   Often   under the webbed foot
    Of my imagining, you   are the entire throng.   Wearing
  your face,   Dust of a brick.   what's left is   What when
the particle accelerator   paints its   disastered portrait

76

iv.   scatter

many phrases starts with shatter.   , crossing
        the parking lot, my skin   pixilated in the sodium light,
harsh corundum   skin a vapor trail   edging
    the slipstream.   Tidy up the floorboards.   the wiggling
infrastructure of a signature.   .   says, I've been here
        before   All airs as if a unified field.   of
    night.   of   Claire.   Collapse, arrangement
        of bones   where the elephant toppled.   spells are cast,

Luster in clusters,   stone I toss   Chicago,
the old ferry   through the house's eye, through the firmament   Light
    bulbs wilting,   carnations flickering,   Like a cyst the crick
dribbles outward   toward   a shore   my lady trickles,
my lady pours   Give up give up,   my sweet canteen
Been taken to the forest.   Honey.   Among the wild fission.

77

OTHER CENTERS OF COMMUNICATION

Point south through winter the satellites'
catch of broadcasts.
                      No heron reside here,
and your abandonment is for heron country.

These avenues retain me, my body, built of echo,
for playing strings.

  I don't have any memory handling a cello,
      though my fingers callus, a chrysalis,

a swirl like stereo speakers.

               Touching, I quiver.
I shudder the baseboards.

      See you, you say, aborting
the *I* and the *will* and *again,* the dish of your eye
averted.

     Open-mouthed, I raise my hand
and gesture good night.

A static lingers then that no antenna collects.

It's made from the gaps in language.
     And language is made from heat.

What compressed air simmers over asphalt
enters the throat and speaks.

What in the lamplight gurgles,
in morning in moth sleep settles.

No transmission can convey me.

I am standing in a clearing.
I am bothered about beauty.

NOTES

"Transmission from HQ" owes a debt to the album *Yankee Hotel Foxtrot,* by Wilco.

"Employing My Scythe" is for Mike Anichini.

"All the Hexagonal Faces Lilting from the Crowd" is for Rachel Richardson.

"From *The Tractatus Logico-Philosophicus,* Unabridged" contains excerpts from *The Tractatus Logico-Philosophicus,* by Ludwig Wittgenstein, as translated by C. K. Ogden.

"Profane Portraiture" is after "Postcard" by Olena Kalytiak Davis.

"Pruning the Dead Tree" takes its inspiration from the line "at least I have not woken up with a bloody knife in my hand" in the poem "Self-Portrait at 28," by David Berman.

"Mood Ring" is for my father.

"Auto Immune" is after Dean Young.

"Inspired by Actual Events" is actually inspired by James Tate.

"Carrier Wave" is for Brenda Hillman.

"Operating Dictates for a Particle Accelerator" owes a debt to the album *Brighten the Corners,* by Pavement.

"Other Centers of Communication" takes its title from a line in John Ashbery's "And *Ut Pictura Poesis* Is Her Name" and is after that poem.

ACKNOWLEDGEMENTS

Inexpressible gratitude to my aunt and uncle for nothing short of parental devotion and to my cousins Sandie, Parminder, and Pardip Bolina for being nothing less than siblings

Thanks to the editors of the journals in which some of these poems previously appeared: *Laurel Review,* "What Awaits the Thunder" and "Inspired by Actual Events," and *Ploughshares,* "Employing My Scythe"

Thanks to the following friends, writers, and mentors for their support, encouragement, and guidance: Jon Bishop, Matt Brett, Paul Levi Bryant, Jackson Connor and traci o connor, Jeff Courtright and Linn Healy, Phil Crymble, Ned Fluet, Alice Fulton, Matt Greaney, Linda Gregerson, Mark Halliday, Terry Hanson, George Hartley, Robert Hass, Brenda Hillman, Ray and Monica Kouza, Laura Krughoff, Megan Lobsinger, Tom McGettrick, Thylias Moss, Michelle Mounts, Rachel Nelson, Anne Ozar, Rachel Richardson, Jorge Sanchez, Catherine Taylor, Keith Taylor, Antoinette Ursitti, Pete Vanaria, Dave Wanczyk, Mike Wright, Sharmila Voorakkara, my cohort at the University of Michigan, and the Tennessee Stud, Richard Tillinghast

Thanks to Stephanie G'Schwind and the folks at the Center for Literary Publishing at Colorado State University for taking such care in the publication of this book

Thanks to Lyn Hejinian for choosing this book to be published

Special thanks to Ray McDaniel, poet and editor extraordinaire

Unending gratitude to Dean Young for getting me started

and to my tribesmen Michael Anichini and Noah Montague, *thanks* is too small a word